Mum's the

A play

Brian Miller

Samuel French—London
New York-Toronto-Hollywood

ISBN 0 573 12172 9

CHARACTERS

Jessica, early/mid-40s, sophisticated, svelte
Grantham, 65, ex-army officer, dull stick, wary
Aunt Herbacia, 80, not wholly 'there'
Geraldine, 30, unfeminine
Amelia, 50s, transatlantic, over-bejewelled
Detective-Sergeant Hoskins, C.I.D., 30s, rough
    diamond

Note on setting: Most of the action takes place at the secluded and pleasant Artichoke Cottage, somewhere in the Home Counties, in the late summer/early autumn in the present. The main acting area of the stage is divided in half: the stage right is the sitting-room of Artichoke Cottage, leading by means of a pair of french windows (at a right angle to the audience) to the stage left which is the patio of Artichoke Cottage. A later scene at the local police station takes place at extreme DR.

MUM'S THE WORD

SCENE 1

Lights come up on the patio of Artichoke Cottage. Mid-afternoon. We hear light garden birdsong in the background

Grantham, a retired army officer, sits at the patio table cleaning his revolver. Perhaps he is humming

He looks up briefly and even warily at Jessica, carrying a tea-tray laden with tea-things. She opens the sitting-room french windows and comes through on to the patio

Jessica (*approaching*) What are you doing, dear?
Grantham Cleaning my revolver.

Jessica sets down the tray and puts two cups and saucers on the table

Old service revolver. Thought I'd get it out.
Jessica Oh yes, dear.
Grantham Sometimes a man feels like cleaning his weapon.
Jessica (*pouring his tea*) Take care, Grantham.
Grantham Of course I take care. See? (*He holds up the revolver and twirls the chamber*) Chamber's empty.
Jessica Where are the bullets?
Grantham (*tapping his shirt front*) Keep 'em here.
Jessica No wonder your shirts get shapeless! Take them out at once!

Grantham Yes, dear. (*He takes out six bullets and puts them on the table*)

Jessica Drink your tea before it gets cold.

Grantham Yes, dear.

He drinks his tea. Jessica sits down and drinks her own tea

Jessica We aren't waiting for Aunt Herbacia.

Grantham Bit off-colour today, is she?

Jessica No. I just don't feel like waiting for her.

Grantham Thought she looked a bit off-colour at lunch.

Jessica (*thoughtfully stirring her tea*) I think something needs to be done about Aunt Herbacia.

Grantham (*holding up the revolver and examining it keenly*) So you always say. Hm. Yes.

Jessica What are you doing?

Grantham What? Nothing, Jessie.

Jessica I don't know what's got into you.

Grantham Hm?

Jessica Unkempt. Unshaven. Going to seed generally.

Grantham What? Come now, old girl ...

Jessica Look at you!

Grantham looks consciously down at his shirt-front

Well?

Grantham I had a bath on Tuesday.

Jessica It doesn't matter how many baths you have!

Grantham Er, Jessica, listen. You should try to understand. When a fellow retires from active service he's, well, he's put off his stroke for a bit. The old routine — sort of buckles. I'll be in good form again when I get used to it.

Jessica You retired five years ago, Grantham.

Grantham Takes a bit of a while.

Jessica I haven't retired. I haven't let myself go, have I?

Grantham (*resuming cleaning the revolver*) Let yourself what?

Jessica No, I haven't. I'm still young and gay.

Grantham As fresh as the day I married you!

Jessica Don't overdo it, Grantham.

Grantham Sorry, m'dear.

Jessica I still feel a good part of my life stretching out before me.

Grantham Don't we all.

Jessica Not you.

Grantham What do you mean?

Jessica You're a man. Statistically men die off sooner.

Grantham (*chuckling*) I'm not dying off sooner!

Jessica Oh yes you are.

Grantham Oh no I'm not!

Jessica Would you like to make a wager?

Grantham Now stop this nonsense, Jessie. You're just in one of your moods.

Jessica One of my "moods". Passes the time.

Grantham I must say it's a odd way to amuse oneself.

Jessica Why are you cleaning your gun?

Grantham Revolver. Just something to do. As a matter of fact it gets a bit mucky now and then.

Jessica How can it possibly get mucky? When did you last fire it?

Grantham Hm ... Nineteen-fifty-two?

Jessica Nineteen-fifty-two. And was it fired in anger?

Grantham You've got me there. Quite honestly I don't remember.

Jessica You don't remember?

Grantham A long time ago! Hell of a long time ago.

Jessica I have no recollection of nineteen-fifty-two myself.

Grantham I wish I knew what was bothering you.

Jessica I'm bored, dear.

Grantham What on earth have you got to be bored about?

Jessica One doesn't have things to be bored *about*. That's half the trouble.

Grantham I don't know how you can be. Here we are. Lovely cottage. No neighbours for miles about in all directions, idyllic.

Jessica I know, boring.

Grantham My gosh, if you'd ever been in a P.O.W. camp —

Jessica But I wasn't. And neither were you.

Grantham Corky Simmons was.

Jessica I don't want to talk about Corky Simmons. I'm bored to distraction. Something has to happen soon or I'll go out of my mind.

Grantham Something good, or something bad?

Jessica Oh, don't be so obtuse! Bad, of course!

Grantham I suppose you must be talking about a divorce.

Pause. Jessica looks at Grantham in amazement

Jessica Whatever put that idea into your head?

Grantham What? Well ... Everybody's doing it these days, aren't they? Says so in the *Telegraph*.

Jessica Grantham, you've been keeping something from me. You want a divorce!

Grantham No!

Jessica Then why did you bring it up?

Grantham I read about it in the *Telegraph*.

Jessica You were trying to get at something.

Grantham I'm not getting at anything! You're the one who's doing all the getting!

Jessica At any rate I don't think divorce is the answer.

Grantham The answer to what?

Jessica It's out of the question for us, Grantham; who would move out?

Grantham Move out?

Jessica One of us would have to go. It wouldn't be you — you're much too settled.

Grantham I suppose you wouldn't mind going if you're so bored with the old place.

Jessica But I couldn't. Who would look after Aunt Herbacia?

Grantham You could take her with you.

Jessica You *have* thought this out, haven't you? No. She wouldn't be able to leave Artichoke Cottage. She's lived here too long — the move would probably kill her. And there's Geraldine. She can't live out on her own on what she earns at the moment. Except in some awful hostel or other. Is that where you'd like to send your niece?

Grantham I haven't thought of sending anyone anywhere.

Jessica Just like you, not thinking things out properly.

Grantham My dear Jessica. I don't want Aunt Herbacia to go. I don't want Geraldine to go, and I most definitely don't want you to go. Perish the thought! Really!

Jessica Most touching.

Grantham And I don't know how we got into this silly conversation in the first place.

Jessica So divorce is ruled out.

Grantham It was never a serious proposition as far as I was concerned.

Jessica I know, Grantham. It just popped into your head, while you were cleaning that. Surely you ought to have finished by now?

Grantham (*with a flourish*) Yes, there! What do you think, eh? They don't make them like that anymore!

Jessica Aren't you going to load it up?

Grantham Bit risky, don't you think?

Jessica What about burglars?

Grantham We'd never get burglars all the way out here, Jessie.

Jessica Anything could happen in a place like this. One of those gangs could come in the night and tie us all up. How do you think Aunt Herbacia's heart would stand up to that?

Grantham Damn sight worse for her heart if I started shooting.

Jessica Grantham, I'm really worried.

Grantham Oh very well — if you say so.

Grantham inserts the bullets into the chamber and clicks the revolver shut

Grantham There.

Jessica (*holding out her hand*) May I see it?

Grantham Er. Well. (*Reluctantly he hands it across*) Be careful … See that hammer at the top? That's the safety-catch. Whatever you do, don't for heaven's sake pull it back or you'll release it.

Jessica (*taking the gun*) Thank you. (*She looks down the barrel*)

Herbacia enters and makes her way through the sitting-room to the patio

Grantham Don't do that!

He tries to snatch the gun back, but Jessica holds on to it

Jessica You're such a fusspot, Grantham.

Herbacia is at the doorway and starts to approach

Herbacia There you are, my dears. Have you seen my knitting?

Jessica No, Aunt Herbacia, we haven't seen your knitting.

Herbacia I must have left it in my room. Then what did I come down for? Oh yes, tea! (*She sits down at the table*)

Jessica There isn't any left.

Herbacia Oh dear.

Slight awkard pause

Grantham Never mind, I'll stir myself and make a fresh pot. (*He goes back to the house*)

Jessica My goodness. We *are* active today.

Grantham (*from inside the house*) I'll be back in a jif.

Grantham exits R

Herbacia What have you got there, Jessica?

Jessica Grantham's army *revolver*. (*Pause*) Last fired in nineteen-fifty-two.

Herbacia But that was in the war!

Jessica No dear, you're thinking of nineteen-forty-two.

Herbacia But there was a war then! Korea or somewhere. Years before Geraldine was born. You haven't seen my knitting by any chance?

Jessica looks, then reaches across to Grantham's chair with her free hand, picking up Herbacia's knitting

Jessica Thought it was a cushion, I expect. There. (*She hands it to Herbacia*)

Herbacia (*taking the knitting*) Thank you, dear.

Jessica Whatever are you knitting *now*, Aunt?

Herbacia My shroud. I want a nice woolly one, so I won't be cold.

Jessica That's not a very happy joke, is it, dear?

Herbacia I'm not a very happy person, Jessica.

Jessica I'm terribly happy — by nature. Only I haven't found the right outlet as yet.

Herbacia It's not that I'm *unhappy*. In between, really. I suppose it's because I don't have so much to look forward to anymore. But it doesn't matter. (*She begins to knit*)

Jessica No, it doesn't. (*Pause*) Aunt Herbacia, what do you think about change?

Herbacia You mean silver and coppers, dear?

Jessica Don't be deliberately dense. I mean a change of circumstances, a change of life?

Herbacia There's only one important change to come, dear.

Jessica For you, yes. (*Pause*) I've been thinking about Grantham. I don't know if you'll understand, Auntie, but after five years of his retirement I've become so desperately bored with everything I don't know what to do.

Herbacia Have you, dear?

Jessica It was different in the old days. When we were on the move. There were so many nice young subalterns about.

Herbacia We all feel frustrations sometimes, Jessica. Just take each day as it comes. You aren't thinking of doing away with yourself, are you?

Jessica No, not that.

Herbacia It would be very foolish.

Jessica You're coming along well with that shroud.

Herbacia Do you think so? I shan't be wearing it just yet, of course! There's a long time to go still. I've survived everyone else. I expect I'll even survive you.

Jessica That wasn't very tactful, was it, dear?

Grantham comes through the house and into the garden with the fresh pot of tea and an extra cup and saucer

Grantham Here's some more tea.

He pours the tea into Herbacia's cup

Herbacia Jessica's been saying odd things, Grantham.

Jessica I think it's time for you to go upstairs, Auntie.

Herbacia But I've only just come down.

Jessica Chills are so easily caught this time of year. The elderly are especially susceptible.

Grantham But I went to all this trouble to make fresh char.

Jessica Then she can take it upstairs, can't she?

Herbacia gets up, holding her knitting

Herbacia I suppose you're right, dear. One shouldn't stay out here too long. (*She starts to move off*) One never knows where it might lead.

Jessica Quite. (*She holds out Herbacia's cup*) Don't forget your tea.

Herbacia Oh! Thank you! (*She takes it and departs again through the house*) I always knit better indoors anyhow.

Herbacia exits R. Pause

Jessica Grantham, I do think we must face up to some sort of change in our lives.

Grantham You're not still thinking of a divorce are you?

Jessica I wish you wouldn't keep harping on that! We must be sensible. Divorce is out of the question. It's not respectable for people like us. It's messy. In the economic sense.

Grantham I quite agree, old girl. Anyhow I never really thought of you caring much for the idea. Could I have my revolver back?

Jessica We must be serious about this. I hope you'll forgive me for saying so, Grantham, but I think you ought to pass on.

Grantham Pass on? What do you mean, m'dear?

Jessica Die, Grantham. (*Pause*) Please — don't take it badly. It's
got nothing to do with you personally. Well, perhaps in a way,
but — it's not really your *fault*. Frankly I think things would be
better all round if you — well, I mean — if I carried on without
you. Do you understand what I'm saying?

Grantham I'm not sure if I do, actually.

Jessica I'm putting it very badly.

Grantham No, not at all. I'd like you to think that I keep an open
mind on these things, Jessie. (*He stands and reaches across for
the revolver*) Now if I could just have ...

*Jessica quickly rises and backs away from Grantham, pointing
the revolver at him. She releases the safety catch. Grantham gives
a heavy, despairing sigh*

Jessica You're being very sweet about this. I knew you'd
understand really. When all's said and done I've been quite
fond of you, you know.

Grantham Kind of you to say so, Jessie. (*Pause*) It's been — a
good marriage, don't you think?

Jessica I don't know as I'd go so far as *that*, but even if you think
it has, all good things must come to an end, mustn't they?

Grantham You've looked into the financial aspect, I suppose?

Jessica I'm not that desperate — I've plenty of money of my
own, as you well know. So a death certificate for the sake of a
half-pension doesn't concern me. Anyhow your *full* pension
was a joke.

Grantham I guess you know what's best.

Jessica Good God, if you're going to stick up for yourself now's
the time to do it! Oh, if you weren't such a doormat I might not
have to be going through with this!

Grantham I haven't always been the man you thought I was, you
know.

Jessica Oh? What sort of man have you been?

Grantham I can't tell you straight out like that. But I've had my moments. Why, once in the army, Jessie, I nearly slept with an ambulance driver. A woman.

Jessica You told me that six years ago.

Grantham Did I? I'd forgotten.

Jessica Well, you're forgiven. I think I forgave you then, as a matter of fact. But we're straying from the point.

Grantham (*sweating by now. Gulping*) Are we?

Jessica I'm young enough for a whole new life. There are things I need to do before I get to be like Aunt Herbacia. Things that can't possibly involve you.

Grantham I hope you're not telling me you've found another man.

Jessica Why is a woman only supposed to do things because of a man?

Grantham Just an idea. Thought you might want me to give way. Sort of an alternative, to, er ...

Jessica There can be no alternative, Grantham.

Grantham But couldn't we just talk about this —?

Jessica There isn't time. Geraldine will be home soon.

Grantham Ah yes, I'd forgotten about Geraldine.

Jessica You know how she needs her tea. How that girl can put it away like that I'll never know.

Grantham I imagine you've given some thought to the police — that sort of thing?

Jessica I suppose I'll cope if the matter arises.

Grantham Too late to think about divorce even now, I suppose?

Jessica Grantham, *please* !

Grantham (*intensely*) It could be discreet! Very discreet! (*Pause. He sighs*) Yes well — that's that. (*Pause*) In spite of everything I shall miss you, my dear.

Jessica What an odd thing to say. Oh! You mean in the afterlife!
I should think you'll find plenty of distractions there, if there is
such a place. It's probably just like your club. (*Helpfully*) I
suppose I ought to ask you if you have any last request?

Grantham No, I don't think so. I thought I might shut my eyes.
You wouldn't consider that unmanly?

Jessica There might be something about to throw over your head
if you'd prefer ——

Grantham No, no, this'll be all right. Would you object to one
last kiss?

Jessica It wouldn't do, Grantham. Rather distasteful in the
circumstances, I think.

Grantham Yes, old girl. You always did know best.

Jessica Shut your eyes, now, there's a lamb.

Grantham (*shutting his eyes tightly*) Goodbye, Jessica.

Jessica Goodbye, Grantham.

*Jessica fires the revolver. With a cry, Grantham instantly falls
back from the impact and lies on his back on the patio. Pause.
Jessica looks at him*

Grantham. Died like a soldier.

Herbacia's voice is heard off R

Herbacia (*off*) Jessica?

Herbacia appears and comes through the house

I heard an explosion! Was it the gas? (*She comes on to the patio
holding her nose*) Goodness, it *must've* been the gas or
something — what a dreadful smell!

Jessica Cordite, dear.

Herbacia almost stumbles over Grantham's body. She looks down at him

Herbacia Gracious, what's Grantham doing on the ground? Is he dead? (*She looks around and coughs*) I think I'll sit down.
Jessica I should.

Herbacia sits down

Herbacia Was it an accident?
Jessica I shot him.
Herbacia That was a bit careless, wasn't it, dear?
Jessica I wasn't being careless, Auntie, I shot him on purpose.
Herbacia Oh, I see. What will you do now? Telephone the police? On the wireless they always telephone the police.
Jessica Why should I want to do that?
Herbacia I don't know, really. I expect it's something to do with being arrested.

Jessica sits down beside Herbacia

Aunt Herbacia, it's time for a little talk.
Herbacia What would you like to talk about, dear?
Jessica You know we have sometimes spoken of the idea of your one day leaving Artichoke Cottage?
Herbacia Not the Home, Jessica! Please, not the Home! I won't be any trouble to you, really I won't!
Jessica They'd take such good care of you, Auntie. And they'd have to, wouldn't they — if I was sent away?
Herbacia Why should you be sent away?
Jessica So let's have no more talk of the police.
Herbacia I admit that was a bit silly. Grantham will be happy,

wherever he is. I shall pray for him.

Jessica That's the spirit. And you've survived him, haven't you?

Herbacia Oh yes, I have. But then I'm going to survive everyone.

Jessica Don't be childish, Auntie. We must put our thinking caps on. We can't leave Grantham out here. Whatever would Geraldine think? He must be laid to rest. But where?

Herbacia Under the loose floorboards in the greenhouse!

Jessica Good grief! However did you think of that?

Herbacia We could dig a hole. A nice deep one so he won't feel the cold in winter. What are we going to tell Geraldine?

Jessica Leave Geraldine to me, Auntie.

Herbacia Do you think she'll split on you?

Jessica does a double-take. She looks slightly alarmed at Herbacia

Jessica We must hope she doesn't.

Herbacia I hope you don't mind me asking, dear, but I wonder if it would be possible to have a funeral?

Jessica Don't you see that's out of the question?

Herbacia I'd so much like a funeral. I've been to all of them so far — I haven't missed one.

Jessica Well, we're not having a funeral, and that's that.

Herbacia I'd *almost* rather go into a nursing-home than bury Grantham without a funeral.

Pause

Jessica Would a little funeral be all right? Just the two of us?

Herbacia Oh no! We must have a proper one. With the vicar, and a cortège and flowers and guests and sherry afterwards.

Jessica fingers the revolver and looks at Herbacia. Herbacia

*looks at the revolver for a moment. Jessica sighs and puts the
revolver on the table*

Jessica Listen to me, dear. Suppose we compromise. What we
shall do is have a little funeral, all of us dressed in black, after
we've buried him. All three of us, when Geraldine's brought
round to the idea. Those nursing-homes can be very horrid —
extremely mean with the central heating in the autumn. You'd
be sure to catch your death. And then *we'd* survive *you*.

Herbacia Yes. Yes, I expect you're right, Jessica.

*Jessica rises and goes over to Grantham. She picks him up by his
feet and starts to drag him across the stage* L. *She lets go*

Jessica Oh Grantham — you're *such* a dead weight! All those
suet dumplings!

Herbacia Is there anything I can do?

Jessica No. Just keep a look-out for callers. Not that we ever have
any, but on a day like today you never know what will happen!
I'll have to fetch the wheelbarrow.

Jessica turns and starts to go off L

Herbacia (*rising from the chair*) I'll make a cup of tea soon. Oh,
Jessie!

Jessica (*stopping*) What?

Herbacia If you're going to be digging do you think you ought
to wear that frock?

Jessica I want to keep cool and this is all I have.

Herbacia If you say so. I'll do supper tonight, dear.

Jessica starts to go off again. Herbacia stops her again

Will Geraldine be at home at her usual time?

Jessica (*sighing*) You know she always rings if she's going to be late!

Jessica starts to go off again. Herbacia stops her again

Herbacia Jessica!
Jessica Now what?
Herbacia I thought we could have omelettes. Would you like two eggs or three?
Jessica Two, Herbacia, as usual!

Jessica exits

Herbacia I think I'll have three, I'm that starved! Oh! It's so exciting, isn't it? (*To the audience*) I haven't cooked a meal since you all came down with influenza!

Black-out

SCENE 2

Later that afternoon

The patio table is set for three. There is bread on a board on the table. The revolver is gone

Jessica approaches from L. Her hands and dress are soiled. She brushes back a lock of hair from her forehead

Herbacia crosses into the patio from R at the same time. She is wearing a pinny. Herbacia and Jessica meet in the patio. They speak quietly, discreetly

Jessica I didn't realize it would take so long.
Herbacia Geraldine's back — she's changing upstairs. I told her

you were gardening. Have you made enough room for Grantham, do you think?

Jessica He shan't lack for home comforts. (*She looks around*) Auntie, I don't suppose you know where Grantham's revolver got to, do you?

Herbacia Oh dear! Yes, I did pick it up, I remember that, when I laid the table. Where did I put it?

Jessica There were fingerprints on it that could be incriminating evidence.

Herbacia Incriminating evidence! I know all about that from the wireless!

Jessica You see how important it is for us to find it, don't you?

Herbacia Oh, I do! I'll have a hunt for it after supper. Sit down now, Jessica. (*She goes into the house*) The omelettes are ready!

Jessica sits at the table and puts her head in her hands. She is exhausted

Geraldine appears in the sitting-room from R. She is wearing a tracksuit. She meets Herbacia in the sitting-room

Herbacia I've done supper tonight, Geraldine!

Geraldine How exciting.

Herbacia It's such a nice evening we're having it on the patio.

Geraldine I was going for a jog first but it doesn't matter — I'm too tired anyway.

Herbacia Now you just have a rest — go and join your Aunt Jessica and I'll bring out the omelettes.

Geraldine Reminds me of when we all had the 'flu. Do you want any help?

Herbacia (*going off* R) No, no! I can manage!

Herbacia exits R

*Geraldine shrugs and wanders into the patio. She's surprised by
Jessica's unkempt appearance*

Geraldine What on earth have *you* been up to?

*Jessica looks up and smiles, as Geraldine takes her place at the
table*

Jessica Just a little digging. Rather a lot actually.
Geraldine You ought to let the old man do the heavy work. I
suppose he's having the usual nap after being totally exhausted
by the *Telegraph* crossword. Gosh, I'm starved. (*Pause*) There
are only three places.
Jessica Your uncle won't be joining us.
Geraldine Woolgathering up at his club, is he?

*Herbacia enters and comes through with a tray on which are
plates with three omelettes. She sets the tray down on the table
and distributes them to each place*

Herbacia Here we are, then!

They commence to eat

Eat hearty, Geraldine.
Jessica (*after a while*) Geraldine, there's something I have to tell
you.
Geraldine Could I have some bread?
Herbacia (*handing the bread board to her*) There you are, dear.
Geraldine Thanks.
Jessica Geradine, I shot your uncle this afternoon.

Geraldine (*choking*) Do what?

Herbacia Right here, on the patio. She sent me away before she did it so I wouldn't be an eyewitness.

Jessica It's all right, Geraldine—there weren't any eyewitnesses and I've buried Grantham nice and snug under the greenhouse.

Pause. Geraldine stops eating and sets her knife and fork down

Geraldine You're serious, aren't you?

Pause. The other two look at her

Wait a minute. Did I hear you right? You say you killed the Major? You killed my uncle? Your husband?

Jessica Yes, dear. I shot him while we were having tea. With his old army revolver. I need to know where it's got to, actually—

Geraldine I don't believe this!

Herbacia Oh it's true, Geraldine! I promised not to tell anyone. We're going to have a funeral.

Geraldine You've both gone round the twist.

Jessica If you mean in the sense of hallucinating I can assure you it's true.

Pause. Geraldine takes this in

Geraldine My God. Poor old Grantham. Major, Army Pay Corps, retired. (*She shoves her plate away*) I can't eat any more. (*She gets up*) In fact what I need is a drink.

Jessica Take the Major's whisky from the sideboard, why don't you?

Geraldine (*going indoors to the sideboard in the sitting-room*) I know where it is. I guess he won't be needing it.

She pours out a stiff whisky, gulps it down, and pours another

Jessica (*calling to Geraldine*) I did it for the best, Geraldine.
  Believe me!

*Geraldine returns with a glass of whisky in her hand. She sits
down again*

Geraldine I'm sure you did. Crikey. (*She takes another swig*)
  Now then. What I want to know is: where does this put me?
Jessica It doesn't alter anything, surely? Except now we can have
  some fun! Take proper holidays! Flirt outrageously with those
  lovely waiters in Marbella!
Geraldine You seem to forget one thing, Jessica darling.
Jessica What's that?
Geraldine What do you *think?* (*Pause*) If I don't turn you in how
  in hell can I go on being a policewoman?

Pause

Jessica The police needn't know, need they?
Geraldine I *am* the police!
Jessica But not *that* sort of police?
Geraldine It's all the same police, Jessie!
Jessica But you aren't police all the time, are you? Not here at
  home with us?
Geraldine I'm expected to enforce the law on or off duty, in any
  emergency.
Jessica But this isn't an emergency, dear. It's all been taken care
  of.
Herbacia You never told us you could make arrests!
Jessica You wouldn't arrest me, would you? I did it for you
  Geraldine. You always found the Major such a bore.
Geraldine If we all went round killing off bores, where would

we be?

Jessica A lot better off in my opinion.

Geraldine (*rising*) I'll have to go and investigate the greenhouse for myself. And if you're telling me the truth, Jessie, well, I'm afraid — I mean I won't have any alternative ——

Jessica (*rising to prevent her*) If you turn me in you'll have to turn in your Great-Aunt Herbacia as an accessory after the fact. She didn't raise a finger to stop me. Or even make it the least bit difficult.

Herbacia I'll be taken to the Home if your Aunt Jessica is arrested.

Jessica Or worse!

Herbacia Worse?

Jessica *Holloway*!

Herbacia Oh no!

Geraldine They wouldn't do that to an old lady.

Jessica Some of those judges can be extremely nasty.

Geraldine The barrister would plead mitigating circumstances.

Jessica Geraldine, after all we've done for you. Brought you up from a baby. Looked after you. Nurtured you. Put you through Hendon. Do you really want to see the nearest and dearest you have in the world hounded into prison for the rest of their lives? Making headlines in all the tabloids? Do you?

Herbacia Will we have to leave the country? They might search for us at the aerodromes.

Jessica No dear. We're not planning an escape, so I don't see the point of all this fuss.

Geraldine *Fuss*? You really are something!

Jessica What do you mean? Why arrest us? They can always find us here if they really want us. There's no hurry.

Geraldine But you can't stay here, scot-free, after murdering somebody!

Jessica Ah, but it's not as simple as that, is it dear? If we were arrested and convicted and came before a judge, he might do anything. He could pronounce me insane — and Aunt Herbacia — and have us shipped off to Broadmoor!

Herbacia Oh no!

Jessica Your own flesh and blood! Pronounced criminally insane! I doubt if such a family taint would do much for your chances for promotion.

Geraldine You're right about one thing. If I turn you in, Aunt Herbacia will certainly have to go into a home.

Herbacia Anything but that, Geraldine!

Geraldine Well I can't look after you, can I?

Jessica It would kill her before her time.

Geraldine Like the Major.

Jessica The Major was a man. All men die early.

Geraldine But don't you see? If I don't do something I become an accessory! I'd have to stand trial too and I'd be booted out of the force!

Jessica As far as I can see, it's only your attitude that makes any difference. No-one will ever know about this otherwise. No-one will miss the Major, poor man. He was the club bore to all his friends — Corky Simmons and the others. They'll be so relieved he's not there they won't wonder what's become of him. Anyhow his club was in London and we're here. We've always kept ourselves to ourselves. He's safely buried under the greenhouse. There's no evidence except for that dratted revolver. If you'll only be more understanding, Geraldine, more interested in the success of your career, no-one need ever know.

Geraldine Why do you have to make things so bloody difficult?

Jessica Why don't you help yourself to more malt whisky? You could never afford that on your pay, could you?

Geraldine looks thoughtfully at her drink, and then at Jessica. The telephone rings off R

Geraldine (*going off to the telephone*) I'll get that. It's probably for me.

Geraldine exits R

Jessica sits down again. Geraldine's indistinct monosyllables can be heard from off R *as she speaks on the phone over the following:*

Herbacia Do you think she *will* turn us in ?

Jessica I don't know. I've never seen this officious streak in her before.

Herbacia Can we have our funeral for Grantham soon, like you said — the three of us?

Jessica If Geraldine arrests us it'll be as large a funeral as you like, Auntie. The trouble is, we probably won't be invited.

The phone is put down off stage and Geraldine reappears and crosses into the patio

Geraldine I've got to get changed again.

Jessica Whatever is the matter?

Geraldine I have to go out.

Herbacia You haven't finished your omelette!

Geraldine You must be joking. There's going to be a big vice swoop and the station needs all the WPCs it can round up to mind the tarts.

Jessica Sounds exciting, dear.

Geraldine Delirious. I don't know how long I'll be. Don't try to leave, either of you.

Jessica (*wearily*) How many times do I have to tell you, Geraldine dear? We have no intention of going *anywhere*.

Geraldine That's all right, then. I'm trusting you. Nothing is to be done until I get back. OK?

Jessica That sounds eminently sensible.

Geraldine exits R

Herbacia Is it curtains for us, Jessica?
Jessica Your guess is as good as mine.

The telephone rings off stage R. *Jessica rises and goes through to it*

Jessica (*calling*) I'll take it, Geraldine! Don't let it hold you up!

Jessica exits R *while Herbacia sits at the table finishing off Geraldine's omelette*

In the course of the following Herbacia pricks up her ears and listens; she gets up from the table and wanders into the sitting-room, listening to the one-sided conversation just by the door. Meanwhile, we hear Jessica's end of the conversation

Jessica (*off stage*) Hallo? Yes. ... Who? ... I'm sorry, I didn't quite — Amelia! Amelia darling, how wonderful to hear your voice! Goodness me. ... You're at Heathrow? My dear, why didn't you warn us? ... A flying visit? ... You're on your way to Israel? How nice. ... Just to see us? But if you're stopping over you must stay the night. ... An hotel. I see. Well, I suppose that's the best. It'll be so lovely to see you after all these years! ... Oh yes, she's the same as always. Older, of course. But you'd never recognize Geraldine! All grown up and everything. ... I don't know whether you will or not, dear, she's going out on a vice swoop. ... A *vice swoop*. ... I don't know: something to do with minding tarts. I'll explain when I see you. How will you get here? ... Hired car, I see. ... Oh dear, your money's run out!

Goodbye for now, Amelia! Goodbye!

Jessica reappears R

Herbacia That was never your big sister Amelia?
Jessica Yes! Isn't it exciting?
Herbacia But she's in America.
Jessica No she isn't. She's here, on the way to a tour of the Holy
    Land but decided to make a stop-over for one night just to see
    us!
Herbacia We ought to air the spare bed.
Jessica She won't be staying the night. What on earth can we
    offer her? She might have given us some warning. (*Pause*) She
    was always like that.

Black-out

SCENE 3

The same day. Evening. Only the sitting-room area is lit

*Amelia is sitting in the centre of the sofa with Jessica and
Herbacia on either side. In front of them is a coffee-table with
three glasses and a port decanter*

*Amelia is heavily bejewelled. She is showing off some of her old
rings. She speaks with an overlay of an American accent, acquired
over many years in the States*

Amelia Thirty-nine dollars! Can you believe it?
Jessica Extraordinary.
Herbacia And this?

Amelia Oh, I just love flashing this one around. It's so opulent! George gave it to me just two days before he passed away. One-fifty-nine ninety-five.

Jessica We were so sorry to hear. He always looked so, well, *comfy* in his pictures. In those sort of tartan shorts.

Amelia Oh gawd. Still. I have to say one thing. He turned out to be worth much more than I thought.

Jessica Really?

Amelia The estate was valued at over three-quarters of a million dollars. Eight-hundred thousand, plus the life insurance.

Jessica You certainly did well by him, dear.

Amelia George always hated to go any place, real stick-in-the-mud. So what do you think? I'm off! Ever since Sunday School I always wanted to go to the Holy Land. You must remember that, Jessie? It's only two and a half thousand dollars, all-in, for three weeks! With another five hundred for Jerusalem and the Wailing Wall! What do you think of that? And the drink's free on the plane both ways! Special offer! (*Pause*) Well, that's enough about me. What about you? (*She hugs Jessica*) My little sister — so gorgeous to see you again, honey!

Jessica Oh, we're ticking along, aren't we, Herbacia?

Amelia (*releasing her*) How's Grantham? Still dishing out the old army pay?

Jessica No dear. He retired. Don't you remember? I wrote to you.

Amelia Of course you did — fancy me forgetting a thing like that. Is he around?

Jessica Around what, dear?

Amelia Around the house? Or has he gone out?

Herbacia Jessica, do you think we should tell her?

Jessica Perhaps we should. She *is* family.

Amelia Oh, do tell all! You have a air of mystery!

Jessica Amelia, it's an odd sort of coincidence your being here but I shot Grantham dead this afternoon. With his old army revolver.

Amelia On purpose?

Jessica Have some more port.

Amelia Just a minute.

She reaches into her handbag and brings out a small electronic device, like a small "Star Trek" phaser. She clicks it on and it buzzes as she runs it over the port decanter. The she switches it off and puts it back in her bag

I should've checked before. Seems OK. (*She laughs*) Better to be safe than sorry! Pour away, then!

Jessica, somewhat puzzled, pours more port into the three glasses. They take the glasses up

Amelia Thanks. Here's mud in your eye, as George always used to say! Go on! Down the hatch! (*She drinks. The others follow suit*) "Down the hatch". Another one of George's expressions. Real original, was my George. Huh! *That* man didn't have an original bone in his body! Boring as an old sweat-sock. Hopeless! (*She takes another swig*) Still, I guess you don't have to be scintillating in the shoe business.

Jessica George was boring, you say?

Amelia Oh gawd! (*She takes another swig*) So you've taken the plunge too?

Jessica Amelia, I'm not sure I know what you're saying.

Amelia I did the same thing. Snap! (*She laughs*) Not with a gun, though. Poison. That's the usual way back home. There's a lot of good stuff on the market these days. The hardware stores are full of it. Just go and buy it, that's all. No permit, no nothing. Stuff for the garden bugs, you know. Take it home and mix it into the garden barbecue sauce. That's what I did. He died right out there on the patio. He had his favourite apron on: "Genius at Work", it had on it. How's that for originality?

Jessica How amazing! Grantham died on our patio.

Amelia George was quite calm until it hit him. And then he didn't know *what* hit him! My feeling is that he sort of departed at the right time.

Jessica But that's what I thought about Grantham! It was the right time!

Amelia Well, there you are, you see. Man gets to a certain age — who needs him? A woman can always be useful, pottering around doing something, but a man, well ... They just get in the way. Especially when you got so used to them being out at work for years and years. George was semi-retired. Spent his afternoons at home. Nearly drove me nuts.

Jessica Grantham was at home *all* the time.

Amelia You had it bad, honey.

Jessica Do you suppose other men's wives have done what we've done?

Amelia (*laughing*) Oh Jessie, sweetheart, you don't know the half of it!

Jessica What do you mean?

Amelia It hadn't occured to me to do anything about George until a few of the girls got together at the club after the aerobics and two or three confessed they'd done it, so that's what gave me the idea! People are doing it all over the place back home! I mean, why not? The only one who gets anything out of a divorce is the lawyer. Who needs it when one trip to the hardware store means your troubles are over? I've never looked back. (*She drinks. Pause*) Anyway, you have to get them before they get you.

Jessica What? ... Oh my God ...

Herbacia What is it, Jessica?

Jessica So that — *that's* what Grantham was doing with his revolver!

Amelia Probably going to make it look like an accident. With George it was knives. He had a whole slew of whopping great knives. Always sharpening them. He said it was for the barbecue meat, but I knew better. They're crafty dear, but they're slow.

Jessica Well!

Herbacia You must be famished, Amelia.

Jessica We've prepared a little supper.

Amelia How sweet of you! (*She reaches into her handbag and brings out the electronic gadget*) Let me check the batteries. (*Sound of a buzz*) Seems OK.

Jessica What *is* that?

Amelia This? Portable electronic food-taster. Tastes everything electronically and clears it for security in seconds. Only fifteen ninety-five mail order. I carry it with me everywhere. Everybody does back home. You never know who's gunning for you, do you? Not that anyone has any reason to do *me* in, but your food sometimes gets mixed up in restaurants. You don't mind, do you? Nothing personal.

Jessica Oh no, dear.

Amelia Better to be safe than sorry. Let's have some more of this stuff before we eat, huh?

They giggle like girls together as Jessica pours. Herbacia picks up the food-taster

Herbacia I've never heard of anything like this on the wireless! (*She holds it gingerly*)

Black-out

SCENE 4

Lights come up at extreme DR

Detective-Sergeant Hoskins sits at his desk talking on the phone. The desk is piled up with paperwork

In the background can be heard the vague, general sounds of a busy police station

Hoskins (*on the phone*) You're telling me we're up to our necks —I shoulda been off more than an hour ago. Yes, OK—where were we? ... What do you mean the evidence is weak? OK, OK, now he's saying he was stitched up, we all know that. Is that it?

Geraldine appears in uniform

Geraldine Sergeant?

Hoskins (*on the phone*) Just a sec. (*To Geraldine*) Yes, what is it, Constable?

Geraldine I was wondering if I could have a word?

Hoskins Be with you in a minute. (*Into the phone*) Look, we have the goods on the villain. Bang to rights! I mean can you beat a guy claiming it was family heirlooms? Pathetic! He was desperate! ... Yes, I know we can't prove that they're *not* family heirlooms. ... Yeah, yeah, a man's innocent until proven guilty and all that bull. ... But if you're not going to prosecute where does that leave *us*? Six months work down the tube, that's what! ... Listen, we acted on suspicion and followed up our enquiries in the usual way! ... O K. ... Yes, whatever you say. We'll keep it on file. ... Thank you and good-night! (*He slams down the phone*) Bloody lawyers! And he stayed up late just so's he'd have the satisfaction of telling me they're not going to bloody prosecute! (*Pause*) Evidence, Constable! Now that's what it's all about nowadays. The courts let 'em in! You've gotta nail these bastards down so hard they can't even wiggle their big toe! Hard evidence, Constable. Facts. Weapons.

Geraldine tries to interrupt as he gets carried away

Fingerprints. Witnesses. Corroborative witnesses. Double corroborative witnesses. If that's how they want to play it, that's how we do it! Work to the rules! Huh! I'll give 'em bloody work to rule! (*He pauses for breath and looks at Geraldine*) Something on your mind? Make it snappy, I got to hear a confession.

Geraldine It's just that I ——

The telephone rings. Hoskins picks it up

Hoskins C.I.D. — Detective-Sergeant Hoskins. ... No, not now. ... Well, why didn't he ——? ... Oh, all right, I'll have to come down and deal with it. Give me half an hour. (*He slams the phone down and pushes the papers around*) How do they expect me to get through this bloody paperwork? Look, Constable, either spit it out or get out. Hey wait, listen — I'm sorry you were roped in on your own time. You know what it can be like around here.

Geraldine You see ——

Telephone rings

Hoskins Bloody hell! Say it now, whatever it is, Constable! Once I pick this up ...
Geraldine No! No, it's all right, Sergeant. Perhaps another time.
Hoskins Suit yourself.

Geraldine exits

(*He picks up the receiver shouting*) C.I.D. — Detective-
Sergeant Hoskins!! ... (*Pause, then subdued*) Oh, yes sir. ...
Press conference? ... Yes, I see. Yes, I can make myself
available. ... Whatever you say sir. ... Did you say tomorrow
at ten? Yes, of course, entirely convenient. ... Thank you sir.
(*He puts down the phone, salutes, touches his forelock, etc.*)
Nothing on then at all, sir! Anything you say, sir! Wash your
car, sir? Think nothing bloody of it, sir!

Black-out

SCENE 5

Same day. Late at night

*Lights come up on the sitting-room—perhaps more subdued and
shadowy than before*

*Herbacia is sitting by herself on the sofa, playing with the
electronic food-taster. She is trying it on an egg which she holds
in her other hand*

Jessica comes in from R

Jessica What are you doing with that?
Herbacia Just testing, dear. This seems to be all right.
Jessica (*pulling the curtains across the french windows prior to
    sitting down*) Amelia will miss that in the Middle East. Where
    did you find it?
Herbacia In the drive when I put the milk bottles out.
Jessica She must've dropped it out of her bag when we poured

her into the car. I do hope she'll be safe driving to Heathrow!
(*She sits down on the sofa beside Herbacia*) Rather leathery
skin she has, don't you think? Must be their climate.

Herbacia I'll put it in my knitting basket for safe-keeping, shall
I? Aren't you going to lock up?

Jessica No, Aunt Herbacia, we won't be locking up! Have you
forgotten Geraldine's not back yet? Really!

Herbacia (*starting to go off* R) Oh, of course, how silly of me. I
think I'll go and check my chocolates. (*She stops in her tracks
and holds up the egg*) Whatever shall I do with this?

Jessica Oh for heaven's sake, leave it there! (*She gestures at the
sideboard*)

Herbacia I suppose so. It's hardly likely to hatch there, is it? (*She
leaves the egg on the sideboard*) Good-night, dear.

Herbacia exits R

Jessica (*calling off*) Geraldine?

Geraldine enters from R. *She goes to the sideboard, looks
around, holds up the egg rather curiously, puts it down,
chooses a bottle, opens it and pours into a glass. She replaces
the bottle and takes a drink*

Geraldine (*making a a face*) Ugh!
Jessica You always did like a tipple after late-night working.

Geraldine looks at the label on the bottle

Geraldine Hungarian brandy? How long have we had this?
Jessica Special offer Grantham picked up. Anyhow, you finished
off the malt whisky and we've just disposed of all the port.
Geraldine Drowning your sorrows?
Jessica Far from it! You'll never guess who showed up — your

other aunt, Amelia, all the way from America! Such a short visit and so much to talk about! I must say they do incredible things over there.

Geraldine Not half as incredible as we do here.

Jessica You'd be surprised. Well, dear, are you going to turn in or turn me in?

Geraldine You know which.

Jessica I thought as much. Your pig-headedness certainly doesn't come from my side of the family.

Geraldine I want you to show me where you buried Uncle Grantham.

Jessica Surely he can keep till morning?

Geraldine No, Aunt. It's time to go for the — (*She coughs*) evidence. (*She coughs and chokes*)

Jessica You'd better sit down.

Geraldine (*perching on the arm of the sofa*) I'm not feeling too good all of a sudden.

Jessica Herbacia should never have attempted those omelettes. She hasn't cooked in years.

Geraldine (*coughing*) My God. (*She coughs again — rasping*) It was the drink, wasn't it? (*Choking*) What — did — you — put — in — the — drink?

Jessica Ant-powder, dear. As much as we had left. We had such a plague last year, don't you remember? I forget to restock.

Geraldine (*strangulated*) Cold-blooded mur—

Jessica But it's all the rage these days, darling. I got the idea from your Aunt Amelia. I'm really very sorry, Geraldine. You weren't a bore like Grantham. But you were becoming just a little boring over this shooting business. Nowadays one doesn't have to put up with people being boring at all. One justs pops along to the ironmonger's and that's that!

Geraldine (*gasping*) You're — mad!

Jessica We're so out of date in this country.

Geraldine (*rushing out of the room* R) I must — try to be sick!

Geraldine exits

Jessica (*looking alarmed*) Perhaps I didn't put enough in.

Jessica rises quickly and goes to the door

Herbacia enters , blocking Jessica's way. Concealed at her side from both Jessica and the audience is Grantham's revolver

Herbacia Where was Geraldine going?

Jessica Off to be sick in the bathroom. I was just going to see that she didn't make a mess.

Herbacia It can't have been my omelettes. My omelettes were perfect.

Jessica (*impatiently*) No, it wasn't the omelettes. I put ant-powder in the brandy.

Herbacia Oh, why didn't I think to check the brandy?

Jessica Will you please stand aside, Herbacia?

Pause. Herbacia holds up the revolver, though not quite pointing it at Jessica. This makes Jessica stop in her tracks

Jessica You found it!

Herbacia You'd never believe where! In my knitting basket! I'm becoming so absent-minded these days.

Jessica I'd say you were a positive danger. Now if you'll just—

Herbacia blocks her way. She has the revolver pointed enough to make Jessica hesitate

Herbacia Only a little absent-minded, but not senile, Jessica.

And I shall survive all of you. I'm not being childish when I say
that.

Jessica Give me the gun, dear.

Herbacia You shouldn't have poisoned Geraldine.

Jessica It's for both our sakes, Herbacia. You don't want to end
up in a Home, do you?

Herbacia I don't care about that now.

Jessica You'd catch your death in a Home.

Herbacia They keep the temperature at a constant seventy-five
in the Glenfield where Hettie Lamprey is. All year round.

Herbacia releases the safety-catch

Jessica Don't do that you stupid old bag!

Herbacia I know all about safety-catches. I heard it on the
wireless. I didn't want Geraldine to die, Jessica. You see,
Geraldine was my daughter.

Jessica What!

Herbacia No-one ever knew, you see. We kept it from everyone
in the whole family! I was over forty, and my Wilfrid was dead
by then. Of course they all thought it was your other sister
Pauline who was having the child. Really, it was Pauline's dear
husband Alfred who made love to *me*. He liked an older
woman, I have to say!

Jessica Herbacia, this is scandalous!

Herbacia Oh, it's all too long ago now, dear. Of course it would
have been a dreadful scandal then. Our secret meetings would
have been found out: Alfred having an affair with his wife's
aunt! In the end we had to let Pauline in on it. That was after she
and I got to Switzerland. She thought it was merely to have a
skiing holiday, not for my confinement! But Alfred persuaded
her that it would be for the best. She hated it at first, but one kept
these things quiet in those days — one didn't have much
choice. They were reconciled, and everyone back home thought

I was nursing her in Switzerland, but of course it was the other way around. Then later, back in England, after Alfred and Pauline died in that terrible accident when the brakes failed, I took care of Geraldine as if she were truly my grand-niece. And that's when she and I came to live with you and Grantham. Geraldine never learned the truth, and neither did you, of course.

Jessica It's quite taken my breath away.

Herbacia I'm not making it up. You could check it in Switzerland if you like. Only it's too late for you to go to Switzerland, Jessica. (*She shouts*) You've killed my only daughter! (*She raises the revolver*)

Jessica Herbacia, I'm terribly, terribly ——

Herbacia fires the revolver and kills Jessica. Jessica falls back on the floor dead

Herbacia Goodness! The recoil!

Geraldine (*calling from off* R) Jessie? Herbacia?

Herbacia It's all right dear, we're in the sitting-room!

Geraldine enters from R, dishevelled and holding a towel. She starts as she sees Jessica's body

Geraldine Oh my God! Herbacia?

Herbacia Yes, I'm the culprit.

Geraldine You'd better give me that.

Herbacia hands her the revolver but Geraldine is shaking

Herbacia You'd better give it back, dear, your nerves are all kaput, which is hardly surprising.

Unprotesting, Geraldine limply yields the revolver back to Herbacia, who puts it on the sideboard. Geraldine stands, as if in a trance. Herbacia bustles about

Thank heaven you're safe.

Herbacia and Geraldine embrace for a long time

Geraldine Oh Herbacia — what are we going to do?

Herbacia Come and sit down. Never mind Jessica for the present.

They sit on the sofa together

Herbacia Now. Are you going to arrest me?

Geraldine (*as if the thought hadn't occured to her*) Arrest you? Oh. (*Dully*) No.

Herbacia Well, that's all right then, dear.

Geraldine I'm resigning from the force.

Herbacia Sounds most sensible, Geraldine. Too many late nights.

Geraldine (*clinging to Herbacia*) You're all I have left.

Herbacia That's true, my dear. We have each other. It should have always been that way. Just the two of us.

Geraldine I've decided I'm going to enter a convent. It came to me while I was upstairs being sick. Something's gone very wrong with the world, Herbacia. I don't want to be a part of it anymore.

Herbacia If that's what you want. Would it be the sort of thing where you'd give up all earthly possessions and wouldn't be allowed to talk?

Geraldine Something like that. I guess I'd be allowed to talk a bit. (*Pause. She gets up wearily*) Come on then. I'm not in a convent yet. We have to decide what to do, don't we?

Herbacia I've just had a thought! We could always say Jessica committed suicide after shooting Grantham! I heard that once in a play! (*She looks at Geraldine*) What do you think? And then — a funeral! A lovely *double* funeral for Grantham and Jessica! Wouldn't that be grand? Do you think they'd allow it?

Geraldine seems too numb to give a response

Geraldine? Would you like it that way?

We leave them standing motionless, with Herbacia looking quizzically up at Geraldine

Black-out

SCENE 6

In the blackness we hear low, solemn organ music

A large spotlight comes up on Herbacia, seated DR, and flanked on either side by a wreath of flowers. She is wearing a black hat and shawl, and clutches a prayerbook

Herbacia Oh! It's so beautiful! They're all dead and gone now. Lovely! Jessica and Grantham. And Maud. And Charles, and Lucy. And old cousin Kemble. I thought he'd *never* go — Geraldine's here, of course. Just the two of us, Geraldine and me. I think a nun's habit will suit her. Much nicer than a police uniform — so much more — *ladylike*. And after she's finished being a novice, and got into the swing of things, she'll be praying away in her convent — out of the world too, really, just like she wanted ... And so I *did* survive you all, my dears ... How long will it be before I see my dear Wilfrid again? I wasn't really unfaithful to you, Wilfrid; the secret meetings with

Alfred only happened after you died ... But that's not why
you'll be cross with me, is it? I could never be an unfaithful wife
to you — at least while you where alive — and after that it
didn't count, did it? *That* was why I *did* it, Wilfrid, so that I
wouldn't betray you. Anyhow, I was sure you'd be happier in
the next world. I do hope you have been ... And my having
Geraldine was the cause of so much anxiety between Pauline
and Alfred! They never really patched it up, and things only got
worse between them. I thought it would all explode and
everyone would find out. That's when I heard something on the
wireless about brake linings. I think it was in a murder mystery.
One of those Saturday Night Theatres on the Home Service ...
Of course it would have been so much nicer if everyone could
have stayed alive, but we can't have it to do over again, can we?
... (*She breathes deeply*) Oh, just smell all these lovely flowers!
Reminds me of the meadow, when he and I — before they built
the housing estate. Oh, long before that ... I wish I could feel
the warmth of that sun again. (*She shivers*) It's gone so cold. I
wonder if they'd notice if I took a little nap? There's no one *to*
notice! (*She puts her head to one side on her shoulder and
closes her eyes*) Yes. Sleep, Herbacia. I feel as if I could sleep
forever ...

She dies peacefully, sitting there, as the Lights fade to Black-out

*The organ-music grows out of her speech and becomes louder. It
then cross-fades into Middle-Eastern Arabic music as the
spotlights come up, extreme* DL, *to reveal Amelia sitting at a
bazaar café table with a jug on it and half-eaten food on a plate
before her. She is rummaging through her handbag*

Postscript

Amelia Oh Christ, where is it? Bloody thing!

She dumps all her contents onto the table and paws desperately through them. Then she seizes her throat and starts to choke

   Ah! Ah! Ahhhhhhhhhhhhhhaaaarrrrgggghhhhh....

Amelia's head falls on to the table and she dies

The lights fade slowly to Black-out. Music slowly fades out

FURNITURE AND PROPERTY LIST

SCENE 1

On stage: Patio table and chairs
Revolver
Knitting

Off stage: Tea-tray. *On it*: 2 cups, saucers and spoons (**Jessica**)
Tea-pot. *In it*: tea (**Grantham**)
Cup and saucer (**Grantham**)

Personal: **Grantham**: 6 bullets

SCENE 2

Strike: Revolver
Cups and saucers

On stage: Patio table set for three
Bread board. *On it*: bread
Sideboard. *On it*: bottle of malt whisky, Hungarian
    brandy and glasses

Off stage: Tray. *On it*: 3 plates. *On them*: omelettes (**Herbacia**)

SCENE 3

| *On stage*: | Sofa |
| | Coffee-table. *On it*: 3 glasses and a port decanter |

| *Personal*: | **Amelia**: handbag. *In it*: small electronic device |
| | (food taster) |

SCENE 4

| *On stage*: | Desk. *On it*: phone and a pile of paperwork |

SCENE 5

| *On stage:* | Egg (**Herbacia**) |

| *Off stage*: | Towel (**Geraldine**) |

| *Personal*: | **Herbacia**: electronic device (food taster) |
| | **Grantham**'s revolver |

SCENE 6

| *On stage*: | 2 wreaths of flowers |

| *Personal*: | **Herbacia**: prayerbook |

POSTSCRIPT

On stage: Cafe table. *On it*: jug and half-eaten food on a
                plate

Personal: **Amelia**: handbag

LIGHTING PLOT

Property fittings required: nil
3 interior, 2 exterior settings

To open: Bring up general exterior lighting on the patio

Cue 1 **Herbacia:** " ... down with influenza!" (Page 16)
Black-out

Cue 2 To open Scene 2 (Page 16)
Bring up patio lighting and interior lighting on the sitting-room

Cue 3 **Jessica:** "She was always like that." (Page 25)
Black-out

Cue 4 To open Scene 3 (Page 25)
Bring up sitting-room lighting

Cue 5 **Herbacia** holds the food-taster gingerly (Page 29)
Black-out

Cue 6 To open Scene 4 (Page 30)
Bring up interior lighting at extreme DR

Cue 7 **Hoskins:** "Think nothing bloody of it, sir!" (Page 32)
Black-out

Cue 8 To open Scene 5 (Page 32)
Bring up more subdued interior lighting on the sitting-room

EFFECTS PLOT